Organisation *of* Nutritional Support in Hospitals

Nutrition steering committee and nutrition support teams -
needs, structure and roles

A Report by a Working Party of the

British Association for Parenteral and Enteral Nutrition

D B A Silk (Chairman and Editor)

TK Cottam, MS Nielsen (Members)

C Elcoat, H Fawcett, KM Furness, JP Howard, JE Lennard- Jones,
CE Plester (Contributors)

Published by The British Association for Parenteral and Enteral Nutrition (BAPEN)
PO Box 922, Maidenhead, Berks, SL6 4SH

Printed by ADM & C Ltd, Biddenden, Kent

ISBN 1 899467 00 9

A CIP catalogue record for this book is available from the British Library.

Available from : BAPEN
PO Box 922, Maidenhead, Berks, SL6 4SH

BAPEN is a Registered Charity No. 1023927

Other reports available from BAPEN:
King's Fund Report -
A Positive Approach to Nutrition as Treatment ISBN 1 85717 016 4
BAPEN - Enteral and Parenteral Nutrition in the Community - ISBN 1 899467 05 X

Published November 1994

The British Association for Parenteral and Enteral Nutrition (BAPEN) was formed in 1992 as a result of recommendations made by the King's Fund report "A Positive Approach to Nutrition as Treatment". The Association is a registered charity.

The Association's aim is to improve the nutritional treatment of all sufferers from illness who have become, or are likely to become, malnourished and who are unable to consume or absorb normal food in sufficient quantities to effect recovery.

To foster this aim the association will:

- Set standards of clinical practice in nutritional support

- Educate and train health care workers, patients and policy makers in the prevention of malnutrition during illness.

- Promote research

This report attempts to address some of the issues raised in the Kings Fund Report.

Contents

Contents (cont.)

Summary of findings

■ Malnutrition in diseased patients delays recovery, increases the incidence of serious complications and significantly increases treatment costs.

■ While the most cost-effective approach to overcoming malnutrition is to encourage patients to eat more normal food, it is not always possible to achieve this and in such cases nutritional support via oral supplements, enteral tube feeding or parenteral nutrition can radically improve recovery rate and quality of life.

■ Over two-thirds of UK hospitals currently have no formal nutrition team responsible for organising the diagnosis, treatment and monitoring of malnutrition in at-risk patients, and in hospitals that do have a team, some only cover parenteral nutrition and some operate only in specific specialties such as surgery.

■ There is good evidence that there are significant benefits where a fully operational multidisciplinary nutrition support team is established; reduction in catheter complications, metabolic complications and morbidity, improved achievement of prescribed goals for nutrient intake and clinical outcomes, and reduced hospital stay arising from the above benefits, plus the implementation of home nutritional support services.

■ These improvements can have significant associated cost savings.

Recommendations

■ All patients in UK hospitals who are diagnosed as being malnourished or at risk of developing malnutrition should have access to a nutrition support team.

■ All patients who are at risk of being malnourished should be routinely screened for malnutrition either prior to or on admission to hospital.

■ All major UK hospitals or hospital groups should appoint a Nutrition Steering Committee (NSC) to be responsible for setting standards for and delivery of catering services, dietary supplements and nutritional support.

■ All NSCs should appoint at least one Nutrition Support Team (NST) to implement the standards of nutritional support laid down by the NSC.

Introduction

It is now nearly 20 years since attention was first drawn to the high prevalence of malnutrition in hospitalised patients and yet the prevalence remains high. Malnutrition has financial implications as well as clinical ones. It complicates illness, delays recovery, resulting in prolonged hospitalisation, and increases the need for high-dependency nursing care and sometimes intensive care, all of which have serious financial consequences.

Advances in medical science have produced methods of providing nutritional support both to improve and to maintain the nutritional state of patients and thus prevent the onset of malnutrition-related complications. Despite these advances, and the proven efficacy of nutritional support in both clinical and financial terms, the nutritional care of patients throughout the UK is fragmentary and poorly organised. There is now very good evidence that this can be improved by adopting a team approach to nutritional management. However, the practical obstacles to setting up multidisciplinary Nutrition Support Teams (NST) may be considerable. There will be both financial and political difficulties but we anticipate that the greatest problem will be persuading consultants and managers that the creation of an NST is necessary.

It is in anticipation of these problems that this working party advises the setting up of Nutrition Steering Committees (NSCs). The initiative for this can be taken by any of the people suggested below as members or a consortium of them. It is hoped that this document will persuade managers that not only will patient care improve as a consequence of the creation of an NST or NSTs within their hospital or district, but that they will also save money.

Once the Nutrition Steering Committee has been formed and the consultant who will lead the NST has been identified, key negotiations with consultants, senior nurses and managers can begin. Evidence that NSTs are feasible comes from surveys of the clinical practice of nutrition support in the UK. Moreover, at a time of great changes in management structures in the NHS, there has already been a clear (albeit small) increase in the numbers of NSTs established over a three-year period.

Malnutrition and its consequences

Clinical

Clinical surveys on hospitalised patients continue to show an unacceptably high incidence of malnutrition in medical, surgical, paediatric and care-of-the-elderly wards.[1-4]

The malnourished patient becomes apathetic and depressed and this may lead to loss of morale and loss of will for recovery. Inability to concentrate means that patients cannot benefit from instruction about techniques needed for self-care. A general sense of weakness and illness impairs appetite and ability to eat.

Loss of power precedes loss of muscle tissue and return of power is more rapid than replacement of tissue.[5,6] Weakness affects the respiratory muscles,[7] making it difficult for a patient to cough and expectorate effectively, with a consequent liability to chest infection;[8] impaired ventilatory drive may also make it difficult to wean a critically ill patient from a ventilator.[9] Cardiac function is impaired, with reduced cardiac output and liability to heart failure.[10] Mobility is reduced, delaying recovery[11] and predisposing to thromboembolism and bedsores.[12]

The malnourished patient develops impaired resistance to infection, which in turn can further worsen nutritional status.[13] Protein calorie malnutrition can lead to altered structure of the small intestine[14] and malabsorption of nutrients,[15,16] which may develop as a consequence of the mucosal lesion as well as of associated exocrine pancreatic insufficiency.[17] Protein calorie malnutrition may have a deleterious effect on the gut immune system[18] and animal studies suggest that it can also lead to alterations in gut barrier function with increased translocation of bacteria from the gut to the mesenteric lymph nodes.[19]

Malnutrition in disease is thus an insidious factor which prolongs recovery, increases the need for high-dependency nursing care and sometimes intensive care, increases the risk of serious complications of illness and, at its worst, leads to death either from a preventable complication or from inanition. These effects of malnutrition have been shown among medical,[20-22] general surgical[20,23-26] and orthopaedic[11,27] patients and among the elderly.[4,28]

Financial

The average length of hospital stay of malnourished patients admitted to a general medical unit was five days longer than those who were not malnourished and resulted in a doubling of hospital charges.[29] A further study of the economics of malnutrition in the hospitalised patient showed that the admission of a malnourished patient who experienced a major complication cost four times that of a normal patient whose disease course was uncomplicated.[20]

Benefits of nutritional support

Clinical

The deleterious effects of malnutrition on various bodily functions have been discussed above. Recent research has shown the benefits of nutritional support. Thus, clinical studies have shown that nutritional support leads to improved wound healing,[30] improved immune response,[31] improved muscle strength, including skeletal,[32,33] respiratory[33] and cardiac muscle[10] and a reduction in postoperative complications.[34-36]

Recent controlled clinical trials have demonstrated short- and long-term clinical benefits of enteral nutrition in orthopaedic[11,37] and geriatric patients[38] as well as those patients with liver disease[39] and Crohn's disease.[40] The clinical benefits of enteral nutrition have also been shown in multiple system trauma[41] and ITU patients as well as in those undergoing major to moderate gastrointestinal surgery.[32]

The indications for instituting parenteral nutrition have been defined[42] and in paediatric and adult patients with intestinal failure it is life-saving. This includes short- and long-term use both in hospital and at home. There are controlled clinical trials supporting the efficacy of parenteral nutrition in postoperative patients,[35] and the role of preoperative parenteral nutrition has now been fully characterised.[36]

Nutritional support must therefore be considered to have an important role in overall patient management. In the severely ill patient it buys time for definitive treatment of the underlying disease to take effect. Nutritional support as outlined below is furthermore cost-effective and in terms of revenue control represents a saving.

Financial

Two analyses of the cost-effectiveness of nutritional support have emphasised the importance of a reduction in the incidence of complications and thus the length of stay and cost per day[43,44] of in-patients undergoing moderate to major gastrointestinal surgery. Up to £450 per patient admission can be saved merely by prescribing oral dietary supplements in the postoperative recovery period (Appendix 1). An estimate undertaken by a recent working party into the role of nutritional support in hospital and at home was based on the assumption that its provision would result in a five-day reduction in hospital stay for 10% of hospital in-patients.[45] In such a model £266 million would be saved annually in the UK (Appendix 2).

Methods of providing nutritional support

It is clear from the above discussion that malnutrition not only complicates illness but has severe cost implications. It is also, in many circumstances, avoidable. These are the persuasive arguments for the nutritional care of the patient being considered at every stage of his/her treatment. A number of ways of providing nutritional support have evolved over recent years.

Normal food

The simplest and safest way of providing nutritional support is to get the patient to eat more. This requires close collaboration between the patient, nursing, dietetic and catering staff. Centralised hospital catering makes it difficult to provide purpose-cooked meals or frequent snacks and the disappearance of the ward kitchen has not helped. Moreover, some food-handling legislation has had a significant impact on what can be provided at ward level.

Oral dietary supplements

These are available in liquid or semi-solid form and, when properly prescribed, can bridge the nutritional gap. Food technologists are working hard to improve palatability, presentation, nutritional formulation and variety. For patients who can swallow liquids, but not solids, oral dietary supplements or nutritionally complete drink feeds are becoming available. The latter are likely to assume a more important role in the future.

Enteral nutrition

If gastrointestinal function is sufficient and the above methods fail to ensure sufficient nutrient intake, nutritional support can be administered enterally via tube feeding. The technology of enteral tube feeding has advanced greatly in the last decade, so that patients can now be fed via a number of routes - nasogastric, nasoduodenal/jejunal jejunostomy and percutaneous endoscopically placed gastrostomy. A wide range of nutritionally complete liquid enteral tube feeds is available and about three-quarters of all hospitalised patients requiring nutritional support can be fed enterally.[46]

Parenteral nutrition

When it is impossible to provide nutritional support via the enteral route the nutrients have to be infused parenterally. Parenteral nutrition can be administered in the short term via a peripheral vein but when required for more than about seven days is generally administered via a central vein. The practice of parenteral nutrition requires the multidisciplinary skills of clinicians, nurses, pharmacists and the Chemical Pathology Department, with the assistance of dietitians. When organised properly it is a safe and effective means of administering nutritional support to the severely ill patient with intestinal failure. Without structured organisation, however, the dangers and complication of parenteral nutrition may outweigh its advantages.

Organisation of nutritional support

Current situation

In the last two decades the use of enteral and parenteral nutrition has gained widepread acceptance. As a consequence, the indications and contraindications for nutritional support have become better understood. At the same time the range of techniques available for optimal administration has widened and become more sophisticated. At present, however, few guidelines are available in the UK as to when nutritional support should be instituted and 'standards' of practice have not yet been agreed at a national level. Moreover, it is only in the last few years that efforts have been made to overcome the lack of education in this area. The resulting enormous increase in available information about nutritional support makes it difficult for individual clinicians who use such techniques only occasionally to provide optimal nutritional management according to the principles of 'best documented practice'.[47]

There is persuasive evidence from two recent surveys into the practice of nutritional support in hospitals in the UK[48,49] that there is a serious lack of organisation in at least two-thirds of hospitals. In some of these the nutritional care of patients appears to suffer from division of responsibility, with catering managers doing their best on a relatively small budget (£11-£14.50 per patient per week) and having little direct liaison with the dietetic department. Many doctors regard malnutrition as a nursing problem, while nurses tend to refer responsibility to dietitians, who in turn have tended to work in relative isolation. None of the above have interacted much with pharmacists, who are now increasingly involved in the preparation and supply of nutrient preparations, or with medical equipment or supplies departments, which provide equipment and disposables for parenteral and enteral feeding.

Development of the team approach

The widespread use of parenteral nutrition and the identification of complications relating to catheter insertion, infection and metabolic abnormalities[50-56] led to the formation of specialist teams with responsibility for parenteral nutrition. These developments took place in several major units in the early and mid-1970s and, as a consequence, it was found that the adoption of stricter protocols of care and active involvement of specialists with greater experience of the techniques reduced the incidence of complications.[50,56-60] Following the establishment of the early Nutrition Support Teams (NSTs) a number of important studies have been published supporting their continued existence in clinical terms and suggesting that they should be established in all hospitals throughout the UK. This evidence is summarised below. It should be emphasised, however, that the advantages of developing a multidisciplinary team approach to nutritional support should not be measured simply in clinical terms. The patient can be reassured that his/her nutritional care is being supervised by experts who can explain and emphasise the importance of nutrition not only during the patient's illness but also after discharge and in the long term.

Benefits of a coordinated team approach

Catheter-related sepsis

The early evidence that the introduction of an NST significantly reduces the rate of catheter-related sepsis has been confirmed.[61-63] The only case where the introduction of an NST failed to improve infection rates dramatically was explained by the lack of any formal protocol for catheter care at the centre involved - a key role for the NST.[64] The employment of a senior nurse with a special interest in nutrition to supervise catheter care resulted in a significant reduction in catheter-related sepsis, in one study from 33% to 4%[65] and in the other from 24% to 0%.[66] The potential cost-saving to a hospital of a reduction in catheter infection rate in patients receiving parenteral nutrition is summarised in Appendix 3.

Catheter insertion complications

Potential complications of catheter insertion include pneumothorax, hydrothorax, damage to major veins, arteries, brachial plexus and thoracic duct, malposition and catheter or air embolism. Controlled studies have shown that NST-managed patients had a lower incidence of catheter insertion problems[67,68] than patients managed by their supervising clinicians. Moreover, fewer catheters were removed for suspected sepsis in NST-managed patients. This is of particular relevance because unnecessary early removal of a central venous catheter necessitates reinsertion, a procedure which itself has a complication rate of up to 5% even in experienced hands.[69]

Metabolic complications during parenteral nutrition

A number of studies have clearly shown that the incidence of parenteral-nutrition-related metabolic complications is reduced in NST-managed patients compared to those managed by their supervising clinicians.[67,68]

Enteral feeding

The advantages of NSTs are not restricted to parenterally fed patients. NST management reduces morbidity and optimises nutrient delivery in enterally fed patients.[70] Mechanical, gastrointestinal and metabolic abnormalities were all lower in those patients managed by NSTs and, importantly, more of them achieved their energy intake goals.

In the future, the increased use of enteral feeding in immune-suppressed patients (intensive therapy, transplant, HIV/AIDS, oncology) may result in more episodes of enteral-nutrition-related infection.[71] The precautions and standards of care required for patients on enteral nutrition are similar to those for parenteral nutrition and NSTs are in the best position to supervise them.[72]

Cost benefits of NSTs

The cost benefits of NSTs have been clearly demonstrated.[73] They occur as a consequence of more rational prescribing:[74] the NST is likely to encourage the appropriate use of enteral rather than parenteral nutrition.[75] Similarly, the NST may achieve a reduction in the number of days on parenteral nutrition[76], the avoidance of catheter-related sepsis[77] and rationalise supply of feeds and equipment.

Control or advice?

There is new evidence that NSTs can decrease the length (and therefore cost) of hospitalisation[78] and, additionally, that nutritional goals for calories and nitrogen requirements are more likely to be achieved by NST-managed patients.[79] Overall, there is also important evidence that a team that controls and supervises enteral and parenteral feeding provides a better quality of care than a team which advises only.[68,70]

Implementing nutritional support policies

BAPEN recommendations

The Council of the British Association for Parenteral and Enteral Nutrition accepts that the evidence outlined above justifies the establishment of multidisciplinary Nutrition Support Teams. It recognises that the creation of a multidisciplinary team approach will result.

The Council recognises that the multidisciplinary approach has to be flexible and that the team approach should be developed in ordinary adult and paediatric wards as well as in intensive therapy units, which may involve the establishment of more than one NST within each hospital. Given widely varying hospital management structures and clinical roles of different hospitals, the Council realises that local difficulties are likely to occur both in setting up nutritional support teams and in monitoring their activities. To overcome these problems, the Council recommends that a two-tier structure should be established in each hospital for the purposes of managing the nutritional care of patients (Figure 1), with the Nutrition Support Team(s) reporting to a Nutrition Steering Committee (NSC).

Figure 1 Organisation of artificial nutrition support in hospitals

Executive director

Nutritional Steering Committee (NSC)
Business Manager
Chief Catering Officer
Consultant Clinician (Director of Nutrition Support Team (NST)
Director of Nursing
Senior Hospital Pharmacist
Senior Hospital Dietitian
Nutrition Nurse Specialist

Nutritional Support Team (NST)	Commitment
Consultant Clinician (Director)	up to 3 sessions/week
Member of junior medical staff (Registrar/Senior Registrar)*	2-3 sessions - week
Nutrition Nurse Specialist (G Grade)*	full-time
Dietitian (Senior 1)*	part-time
Pharmacist (Grade D)*	part-time
Chemical Pathology Department member	part-time
Microbiology Department member	part-time

* Minimum recommended staff grades

Nutritional Steering Committee (NSC)

Composition

The Council recommends that an NSC is appointed by the Executive Director of each hospital. The composition should be:

- A Business Manager appointed by and responsible to the Chief Executive
- A consultant clinician who will be the Director of the Nutrition Support Team. In the event of there being more than one nutrition support team within the hospital, the clinical directors of the other(s) will also be appointed to the NSC.
- The Senior Hospital Pharmacist
- The Senior Hospital Dietitian
- The Director of Nursing
- The Chief Catering Officer
- Nutrition Nurse Specialist

Philosophy

The NSC bring together representatives of medical staff from all disciplines involved in the nutritional care of the patient. Importantly, it provides for the first time an opportunity for dialogue between managers, clinicians, catering officers, nurses, pharmacists and dietitians. It is recommended that the NSC meets at least twice a year.

Most patients are fed by hospital food. Thus the first priority of the NSC will be to provide a multidisciplinary approach to ensuring the provision of good food that is delivered with suitable speed to the patient, is palatable, is in the right form (eg solid, semi-solid) and is served in an attractive manner, and to ensure proper records of consumption are kept. At least 10% of hospitalised patients need nutritional support and the second priority of the NSC is that this should be properly provided to all patients who require it.

Responsibilities

The NSC will be specifically responsible for:

- Submitting to the Chief Executive business plans for catering and nutritional support
- Negotiating and managing the catering and nutritional support budgets
- Liaising with the Regional Director of Public Health to ensure that the hospital purchasing authorities include contract specifications for hospital catering and nutritional support

- Ensuring that standards for hospital catering and nutrition support agreed by purchasing authorities are adhered to
- Setting standards of nutritional assessment so that malnourished patients are recognised
- Developing protocols for the action to be taken when a patient is found to be malnourished
- Establishing Nutrition Support Teams
- Ensuring that a satisfactory system of patient referral is established within the hospital
- Agreeing standards for nutritional support (which may be those recommended by BAPEN, modified if necessary to suit local needs) and for catering
- Implementing an agreed process of audit for catering and nutritional support (It will be the responsibility of the NSC to determine that the audit process is carried out. With regard to nutritional support, it is recommended that the audit data be suitable for comparable audit, criterion-based audit and adverse account audit. It is further recommended that the method of audit should be standardised in order to be comparable with national and international audit. Audit will be the subject of a future BAPEN Working Party Report.)
- Ensuring that the Nutrition Support Team plays its role in selecting appropriate patients for home nutritional support, training them and providing the necessary physical and psychological back-up, as well as ensuring that their nutritional support is properly monitored

The Nutrition Support Team (NST)

Composition

The Council recommends that the composition of an NST should be:
- Consultant Clinician (Director)
- Member of junior medical staff (Registrar/Senior Registrar)
- Nutrition Nurse Specialist (at least G Grade)
- Dietitian (Senior 1)
- Pharmacist (Grade D)
- Chemical Pathology Department Member
- Microbiology Department Member

Philosophy

In the most recent UK survey into clinical practices in nutritional support,[49] 32.5% of responding district dietitians had access to a formal NST. The teams had been established for a mean of 4.1 years. All included pharmacists and dietitians. Most (92%) included a clinician (of which 86% were consultants), 58% a chemical pathologist, 36% a clinical nurse specialist in nutrition and 30% a microbiologist. These figures serve to illustrate that there is a great variation in team composition in different hospitals, and that membership may be dictated by local circumstances. There seems little doubt, however, that the essential members are a nurse, dietitian, pharmacist and clinician.[76] It is recommended that, even if a microbiologist and a chemical pathologist are not core members of the team, good communications should exist with these two departments. It is necessary to define the role of the NST members as clearly as possible, recognising that there will inevitably be some blurring at the edges rather than sharp demarcation of duties.[80]

Responsibilities (Figure 2)

The NST should first and foremost appreciate the benefits of diplomacy. It is a multidisciplinary team and its members have a major responsibility to discuss all aspects of patients management with their colleagues. As mentioned earlier, there is evidence that a Nutrition Support Team that controls and supervises enteral and parenteral feeding leads to a better quality of care than a team that advises only.[68,70] Difficulties in implementing such a policy can be anticipated in some hospitals. It is recommended that the local Nutritional Steering Committee be responsible for determining this aspect of policy making. In practice, newly formed NSTs are likely to start out in an advisory capacity: if successful, many will develop a controlling and supervisory role.

Figure 2 The role and structure of nutrition support teams

Members of the NST will be responsible for:

- Discussing frequently among themselves and with their colleagues (clinicians, nursing staff, dietitians, pharmacists, chemical pathologists and microbiologists) management of individual cases, and undertaking regular formal multidisciplinary rounds (at least twice weekly)
- Implementing the standards of nutrition support agreed by the NSC
- Monitoring all patients receiving nutritional support - including their clinical, nutritional, biochemical, haematological and fluid balance status; it is important that this aspect of patient management has a multidisciplinary input from all members of the NST
- Managing the budget allocated to it by the NSC
- Auditing its clinical activities - the process of audit will have been determined by the NSC
- Liaising, as individual members, with departmental colleagues (e.g. Pharmacy, Dietetic Department) as well as with medical equipment and supplies departments to ensure that the ordering of parenteral and enteral feeds and ancillary equipment is all properly rationalised and cost-effective
- Following up after discharge severely malnourished patients who received prolonged nutrition support as in-patients - it may be appropriate to establish a special nutrition clinic such as already exists in some centres
- Selecting appropriate patients for home nutritional support, training them and/or their relatives, providing the necessary physical and psychological support and ensuring good communications with GPs and the appropriate community services - the role of the NST in home nutritional support is the subject of a recent BAPEN working party publication[81]
- Fulfilling important teaching commitments: the consultant in charge will be responsible for teaching his colleagues, junior medical staff and, where appropriate, students; the Nutrition Nurse Specialist, dietitian and pharmacist also have a commitment to teach their colleagues, junior medical staff and ward staff
- Participating in research - in each of two recent clinical surveys into the practice of nutritional support,[48,49] 32% of NSTs took part in some sort of research activity. It is envisaged that in future NSTs will perform important research roles, not only locally but through contributions to multicentre trials of nutrition support

Patient referral processes

The care of malnourished patients will only improve if a satisfactory system of patient referral is established. It is recommended that one of the functions of the Nutrition Steering Committee is to ensure that this exists and, because the Nutrition Support Team is a multidisciplinary group, its members can play an important role in making sure patients are referred for nutritional support. For example, ward nurses, dietitians and pharmacists are often in a position to alert colleagues on the NST of developing malnutrition in patients under their care. Successful patient referral will thus depend on a combination of diplomacy, personal relationships and, importantly, the educational role of individual members of the NST within their departments.

Roles of individual members of the NST

The clinician

The clinician(s) on the team must first and foremost ensure that good relations are maintained with non-team clinicians. He/she should ensure that the team's existence and approach to patient care have the support of his/her colleagues. It is recommended that the clinician be of consultant status and act as Director of the team. Although the specialty of the consultant director should be unspecified, he/she should have received training in clinical nutrition and nutrition support practices. If more than one NST is to be established, it is recommended that each be directed by a consultant clinician from the specialty involved (eg paediatrics or intensive care). These clinicians should be appointed by the NSC.

The consultant's clinical experience will enable him/her, in consultation with referring colleagues, to plan nutritional support policies for individual patients. He/she should not only be able to define the most suitable route of administration of nutritional support, but should also take responsibility for regularly discussing the ethics of nutritional support with other members of the NST and his/her clinical colleagues.

The consultant will take responsibility for ensuring satisfactory insertion of intravenous feeding lines and percutaneous endoscopic gastrostomy (PEG) feeding tubes. It is recommended that he/she is assisted in his/her duties on the NST by a registrar or senior registrar who, if adequately trained, may insert such lines and tubes. The specialty of this junior doctor is not specified and sessions should be allocated from existing complements. NST duties will give the junior doctor a wide clinical experience and training in nutritional support.

The clinician will be in a position to ensure that all nutritional regimens meet the needs of the patients and, if significant cardiopulmonary, hepatic or renal failure is present, he/she can advise members of the NST as to whether a specially formulated disease-specific nutritional regimen is required.[46] He/she will take responsibility, in collaboration with the nurse, pharmacist and dietitian, for ensuring that the standards of artificial nutrition support laid down by the NSC are achieved. He/she is also responsible for coordinating the audit process and making sure that the agreed budget is adhered to.

Consultant duties, in addition to coordinating and overseeing the activities of the NST, will also include important teaching commitments involving not only his own colleagues, but also junior medical staff. In recognition of the time involved, it is recommended that up to three consultant sessions be allocated to NSC and NST duties.

The nurse

The nurse on the main NST should be a clinical nurse specialist and be given the title Nutrition Nurse Specialist (NNS). The duties of the NNS transcend ward and unit boundaries. He/she will function within the NST and will be responsible for challenging and consolidating nursing practice to provide the best patient-centred care. This degree of responsibility should be reflected in an allocation of at least a Grade G appointment. If more than one NST exists within an institution the NNS will usually fulfil a similar role on all the teams. Occasionally, however, it may be appropriate to appoint a Link/Associate Nutrition Nurse who is trained in the specialty involved (eg paediatrics) and has an interest in nutritional support in that specialty.

The key tasks and responsibilities of the NNS include:

- Clinical practice
- Education
- Management, including audit
- Acting as the patient's advocate
- Research

Clinical practice

Clinical practice is a key component in the role of the NNS and includes:

- Assisting and training ward nurses in the care of patients receiving nutritional support by applying specialist knowledge to the clinical setting
- Training, counselling and supporting all patients receiving parenteral or enteral nutrition in hospital or the community, and respecting their customs, values and spiritual beliefs

- Acting as a liaison between doctors, pharmacists and dietitians and taking part in the assessment, planning, implementation and maintenance of nutritional support
- Attending nutrition or other clinics to see patients receiving home nutritional support
- Assisting in central venous catheter and PEG tube placement, ensuring that correct techniques are used and correct management is maintained, and, if specially trained, inserting cannulae for peripheral total parenteral nutrition (TPN); advising on and/or undertaking central venous catheter dressings in patients receivingTPN
- Formulating policies and guidelines in order to achieve the highest standards of nutritional care and helping in the selection and design of equipment for nutritional support

Education

It will be the responsibility of the NNS to initiate both formal and informal teaching supported by current research findings in nutrition. The NNS will educate nursing staff and other health care workers involved in the management of artificial nutritional support via access devices. Teaching of patients and families prior to discharge home on nutritional support will enable a level of independent care to be achieved that is both safe and appropriate. This is complemented by teaching programmes supported by written guidelines. The NNS will provide the necessary emotional support during this time and after the patient goes home. The NNS should at all times liaise with the primary health care team in the community responsible for the care of patients receiving home nutritional support, and should undertake domiciliary visits when necessary.

The NNS must remain abreast of current advances in nutrition and should be required to read journals and attend courses and conferences to this end.

Management

The implementation of standards and audit agreed by the NSC are fundamental to the successful management of an NST. The NNS will have an important role in assisting in these processes.

Acting as patients' advocate

The NNS must act in the interest of the patient at all times, providing professional support and guidance. Explanation of plan/procedures in simple terms will provide reassurance for patients. The NNS should liaise with other health-care workers on the NST to ensure that patients' interests are best represented.

Research

There is wide scope for nursing research in nutrition both locally and at a national and international level. Multicentre collaborative studies should be considered so that statistically significant results can be obtained. Critical analysis of results enables current practice to be questioned and thus improvements in quality of patient care to be achieved.

The dietitian

The dietitian has an important role to play on the NST. It is accepted that the contribution of the dietetic service to the successful operating of the NST will be time-consuming. In most instances it is recommended that the hospital's Senior Dietitian be the dietitian on the NST. As with the clinician, it is recommended that the dietitian member of the NST should have received appropriate training with regard to nutritional assessment and artificial nutritional support. This is primarily in order to properly coordinate the activities and contributions of his/her staff at ward level.

The dietitian involved with the NST must achieve a successful collaboration at ward level between the clinicians, nursing staff, patients and relatives. He/she will take responsibility for:

- Assessing nutritional intake
- Assessing nutritional status
- Forewarning clinicians, nursing staff, patient and relatives of the possible need for nutritional support
- Consulting with other members of the NST on the need for nutritional support
- Prescribing and documenting intake of oral nutritional supplements
- Discussing with other members of the NST appropriate access for enteral tube feeding, when indicated
- Discussing with other members of the NST nutritional requirements of both patients requiring enteral nutrition and patients requiring parenteral nutrition
- Monitoring patients receiving nutritional support, in collaboration with other members of the NST, paying particular attention to the nutritional and dietary assessment of the patient
- Collating information about side effects/complications that may occur during enteral feeding, in collaboration with the ward nursing staff.
- Ensuring that agreed standards of enteral nutrition are adhered to, and actively participating in the implementation of the audit process
- Actively promoting the concept of nutritional support through education and training programmes for medical and paramedical staff

■ Liaising, in collaboration with the NST pharmacist member and the NNS, with medical equipment and supplies departments to ensure that the supply of equipment for administering enteral feeding is rationalised; advising about purchasing; and playing an important part in deciding what enteral feeds are used in the hospital

The pharmacist

The pharmacist has a numbers of important roles on the NST. He/she will take responsibility for:

■ Formulating parenteral nutrition regimens for individual patients, in consultation with other members of the NST - he/she is responsible for preparing nutrition solutions and for ensuring the mixture is stable and contains only compatible additives

■ Advising on all problems arising from concurrent drug and intravenous therapy in patients on parenteral nutrition and on pharmaceutical agents available for prolonging venous access

■ Monitoring patients receiving parenteral nutritional support, in collaboration with other members of the NST, and advising about changes in the parenteral nutrition regimen should these become necessary

■ Advising on the purchase of parenteral and enteral products and, in conjunction with the dietitian and NNS members of the NST, liaising with medical equipment and supplies departments to ensure that the supply of equipment for administering enteral feeding is rationalised

■ Playing an important role in the process of auditing nutritional support, particularly in relation to all aspects of parenteral nutrition

■ Liaising with his/her colleagues working at ward level - the ward pharmacist is well positioned to advise the NST of impending malnutrition as he/she will be aware of prolonged prescription of intravenous fluids, multiple prescription of antibiotic therapy, etc.

■ The education of all his/her colleagues in the areas of malnutrition, nutritional support and parenteral nutrition (an important responsibility that follows on from the previous one)

The chemical pathologist

The Chemical Pathology Department has an important role in advising the NST about biochemical monitoring policy. It is essential that a balance is achieved between too little and too much biochemical monitoring - both have cost implications. If a chemical pathologist is not a core member of the NST, a designated experienced member of the Department of Chemical Pathology should be appointed to review the results of investigations performed on patients receiving nutritional support, and this person should attend all review meetings of the NST.

The microbiologist

As with chemical pathology, there must be a close liaison between the NST and the Department of Microbiology. The prompt investigation of fever in a patient receiving parenteral nutrition is a crucial part of patient management. Protocols for the investigation of possible catheter-related sepsis must be agreed and adhered to if unnecessary removal of intravenous feeding lines is to be avoided. The microbiologist has important roles as an advisor on treatment if infection occurs and in the audit process.

Funding and Budgetary Arrangements of Nutritional Support Teams

Introduction

Nutritional Support Teams (NSTs) have been shown to be overwhelmingly cost-effective by reducing the incidence of costly complications, minimising waste, avoiding unnecessary treatments and simplifying the treatments used. Their ability, furthermore, to standardise nutrients and equipment enables bulk purchasing and the negotiation of competitive rates [45]. Against this background, some consideration should be given to the budgetary arrangements for NSTs.

General financial structures will vary widely between hospitals or trusts, but are likely to have a major bearing on the way in which the NST is funded. While these variations make firm recommendations difficult, some broad guidelines may be helpful.

Organisation

Firstly, the NST may be funded as a totally separate entity, or as a sub-unit of another clinical directorate, perhaps that of the lead consultants primary speciality, usually medicine or surgery. In either case, the team should have its own identifiable budget.

Methods of Funding

Two main strategies are available for generating this budget. Firstly, the NST may be funded with a fixed sum provided by simply 'top-slicing' the budgets of the various clinical users. Alternatively, it may be 'zero- budgeted' and acquire its funding by 'selling' its services to clinical users. Both systems have advantages and disadvantages. The 'top-slicing' option is not directly workload-related even though the initial 'top-slicing' will be influenced by work patterns of earlier years. The fact that users have paid a fixed sum for nutritional support services at the start of the financial year will encourage them to seek advice and support for as many patients as possible in order to obtain maximum value for the money. Thus the system may operate to the patients' benefit. The system is vulnerable, however, to changes in patterns of work. As funding is not workload-sensitive, the NST could easily become overspent, particularly as the system encourages referrals. A variation on this option is to revise the budget each year on the basis of projected workload. A further refinement would be to limit users to this workload projection.

With 'zero-budgeting', funding is directly related to workload and so as long as the service is carefully and accurately costed, NST overspending should be avoided. Clinical users may, however, be discouraged from referring patients in order to protect their own budgets and so patients who could benefit from nutritional support might not be referred for the treatment. With such a system, however, it is easier to identify and pass on to purchasers the exact costs of the service. This option is more costly to operate.

Scope of the budget

The scope of the budget may vary from covering just the direct costs of prescribables at one end of the scale to responsibility for all direct costs (e.g. prescribables, equipment and staff costs) and full overheads at the other. It may be more difficult to incorporate the staff costs of a multidisciplinary team of which most members spend much of their time working in other clinical areas. As a minimum, the NST budget should cover prescribables and equipment for which costs are readily identifiable. As well as disposables, the equipment element should also include the costs of capital items such as pumps for intravenous or enteral nutrition since many general ward areas may lack these items.

Budget management

It is very important to identify clearly the budget manager to ensure that control is exercised over both the delivery of user requirements and the financial budget.

Appendix 1: Cost benefits of prescribing postoperative oral dietary supplements

(Calculated from data published in reference 26.)

Length of hospital stay

Control patients	mean	15.9 days
Treatment patients	mean	12.6 days
Difference		3.3 days

ie control patients are likely to spend an extra three days in hospital, at an average cost of £150 per day = **£450 extra**

Complications

Control	Treatment
2 pneumonia	3 wound infection
8 wound infection	

Cost of treating complications (Antibiotic cost = £40; physiotherapy cost = £75)

(2 x £75) + (10 x £40)	3 x £40
= £550 per 20 patients	= £120 per 20 patients
= £28 per patient	= £6 per patient

ie the extra cost of treating complications if no supplement is given
= £(28 - 6) = £22 per patient

Total extra cost if no oral dietary supplement is prescribed

£450 + £22 = **approximately £470 per patient**

Appendix 2: Potential national financial saving from nutritional support of undernourished patients in hospital

(derived from reference 45)

Evidence in this report shows that feeding malnourished patients improves recovery rates, decreases complications, reduces length of hospital stay and reduces cost per day of stay.

Assumptions

10% of UK hospital in-patients[a] could have their hospital stay reduced by 5 days[b].
Each of these patients is fed for 14 days after admission[c]
Average increased cost of feeding is £19 per day[c]
Average in-patient cost is £150 per day[d]
Number of admissions is 540 000[e]

Cost savings

5 days at £150/day   £750

Increased cost of feeding

14 days at £19/day   £266
Saving per patient   £484

National saving for 10% of inpatients

(540 000 admissions)   £266 million

a. Reports have shown that up to 50% of surgical patients admitted[d] and 44% of medical admissions[e] are undernourished. These two patient groups represent 70% of the total number of in-patients. We have assumed 10% of all admissions to ensure that the calculation is based on a conservative assumption.

b. Published figures[11,37,35,83,84] show a range between 5 and 16 days; the lower limit is taken as the most conservative estimate.

c. We have assumed that
   c   65% are sip-fed with 1 litre of 1.5 kcal/ml enteral feed per day
   c   25% are tube-fed with 2 litres of 1.0 kcal/ml enteral feed per day
   c   10% are parenterally fed for 14 days
The average cost per day is £19 including an incremental 1 hour per day of nursing time (nutrients alone cost £7 per day)

d. This is usually quoted as between £100 and £200 per day for general wards and between £500 and £1000 for critical care units. We have assumed an average cost of £150 per day.

e. This figure is based on 2 300 000 medical admissions (minus 15% for day cases), 4 000 000 surgical admissions (minus 25% for day cases) and 500 000 geriatric admissions

Appendix 3: Potential cost saving to a hospital by a nutrition team from a reduction in catheter infection rate in patients receiving parenteral nutrition

(derived from reference 45)

These studies show the proportion of patients receiving parenteral nutrition who developed a catheter-related infection before and after the introduction of a nutrition team.

Infection rate per cent

Reference	Before	After
61	29	4.7
62	24	3.5
63	33	3
65	33	4
66	24	0
67	25	1.3
85	21	1.3
Mean	27	2.5

Assumptions

1. An average hospital unit will treat 69 patients with parenteral nutrition each year
2. The introduction of a nutrition team will save 16 episodes of catheter-related infection each year from the mean figures above
3. The cost of each episode of sepsis lies between £1650 and £5000, derived as follows:

   a) 'Best case scenario' (stay in a general ward increased by seven days, organism sensitive to antibiotic, catheter removed and need not be replaced)

Hospital bed @ £250 per day	£1400
Bacteriology (cultures, antibiotic sensitivity)	£100
Antibiotics	£50
Intravenous fluid disposables	£50
Repeat bacteriology	£50
	£1650

Appendix 3 (Cont'd.)

b) 'Worst case scenario' (stay in a high-dependency unit increased by 10 days, resistant organism needing special antibiotics, catheter has to be removed and replaced)

Hospital bed @ £450 per day	£4000
Bacteriology	£100
Antibiotics	£400
Replace intravenous catheter	£450
Repeat bacteriology	£50
	£5000

(Figures estimates from departments at the Central Middlesex Hospital NHS Trust)

Conclusion

Potential cost saving for a reduction of 16 episodes of catheter infection lies between £26,000 and £80,000.

Appendix 4: Membership of the Working Party

Mr T K Cottam

Divisional Manager

Abbott Laboratories Ltd

Maidenhead

Dr M S Nielsen

Consultant in Charge

Intensive Care Unit

Southampton General Hospital, Southampton

Dr D B A Silk

Consultant Physician / Co Director

Dept. of Gastroenterology and Nutrition

Central Middlesex Hospital, NHS Trust; London

Contributions from

Mrs C Elcoat

South Durham Health Care

Darlington

Ms H Fawcett

Nutrition Nurse Specialist

Chairperson of Working Party of

National Nurse Nutrition Group

Ms K M Furness

Senior Pharmacist

Pharmacy

St. George's Hospital, London

Mrs J P Howard

Head of Nutrition and Dietetic Services

Bristol Royal Infirmary, Bristol

Prof J E Lennard-Jones Chairman BAPEN

Ms C E Plester

Research Dietitian

Department of Surgery

Edinburgh Royal Infirmary, Edinburgh

References

1. Moy RJD, Smallman S, Booth IW. Malnutrition in a UK children's hospital. J Hum Nutr Dietet 1990; **3**: 93-100.

2. Bistrian BR, Blackburn GL, Vitale J, Cochran D, Naylor J. Prevalence of malnutrition in general medical patients. JAMA 1976; **253**: 1567-1570.

3. Hill GL, Pickford I, Young GA *et al*. Malnutrition in surgical patients: an unrecognised problem. Lancet 1977; **i**: 689-692.

4. Larsson J, Unosson M, Ek A-C *et al*. Effect of dietary supplement of nutritional status and clinical outcome in 501 geriatric patients - a randomised study. Clin Nutr 1990; **9**: 179-184.

5. Jeejeebhoy KN. Bulk or bounce the object of nutritional support. J Parent Ent Nutr 1988; **12**: 539-549.

6. Christie PM, Hill GL. Effect of intravenous nutrition on nutrition and function in acute attacks of inflammatory bowel disease. Gastroenterology 1990; **99**: 730-736.

7. Arora NS, Rochester DF. Respiratory muscle strength and maximal voluntary ventilation in undernourished patients. Am Rev Respir Dis 1982; **126**: 5-8.

8. Windsor UA, Hill GL. Risk factors for post-operative pneumonia: the importance of protein depletion. Ann Surg 1988; **208**: 209-214.

9. Benotti P, Bistrian B. Metabolic and nutritional aspects of weaning from mechanical ventilation. Critical Care Medicine 1989; **17**: 181-185.

10. Heymsfield SB, Bethel RA, Ansley JD *et al*. Cardiac abnormalities in cachectic patients before and during nutritional repletion. Am Heart J 1978; **95**: 584-594.

11. Bastow MD, Rawlings J, Allison SP. Benefits of supplementary tube feeding after fractured neck of femur: a randomised controlled trial. Br Med J 1983; **287**: 1589-1592.

12. Holmes R, MacChiano K, Jhangiani SS *et al*. Combating pressure sores - nutritionally. Am J Nursing 1987; 1301-1303.

13. Bristian BR, Sherman M, Blackburn GL *et al*. Cellular immunity in adult marasmus. Arch Intern Med 1977; **137**: 1408-1411.

14. Stanfield JP, Hutt MSR, Tunnicliffe K. Intestinal biopsy in kwashiorkor. Lancet 1965; **2**: 519-523.

15. Mehta HC, Saini AS, Singh H. Biochemical aspects of malabsorption in marasmus. Br J Nutr 1984; **5**: 1-6.

16. James WPT. Comparison of three methods used in assessment of carbohydra absorption in malnourished children. Arch Dis Child 1972; **47**: 531-536.

17. Winter TL, Ogden JM, Lemaner G *et al.* The effect of nasal intubation and intensive nutritional support on total body protein synthesis and gastro-pancreatic secretion. GUT 1994 (in press).

18. Spitz J, Gandhi S, Hecht G, Alverdy J. The effects of total parenteral nutrition on gastrointestinal function. Clin Nutr 1993; **12**(suppl 1): S33-S37.

19. Deitch EA, Winterton J, Li M, Berg R. The gut as a portal of entry for bacteremia: role of protein malnutrition. Ann Surg 1987; **205**: 681-690.

20. Reilly JJ, Hull SF, Albert N *et al.* Economic impact of malnutrition: a model system for hospitalized patients. J Parent Ent Nutr 1987; **12**: 372-376.

21. Anderson MA, Collins G, Davis G, Bivins BA. Malnutrition and length of stay a relationship? Henry Ford Hosp Med J 1985; **4**: 190-193.

22. Weinsier RL, Hunker EM, Krumdieck CL, Buterworth CE, Jr. A prospective evaluation of general medical patients during the course of hospitalization. Am J Clin Nutr 1979; **j32**: 418-426.

23. Windsor JA, Hill GL. Weight loss with physiologic impairment: a basis indicator of surgical risk. Ann Surg 1988; **207**: 290-296.

24. Warnold I, Lundholm K. Clinical significance of preoperative nutritional status in 215 noncancer patients. Ann Surg 1984; **199**: 299-305.

25. Meguid MM, Campos ACL, Meguid V *et al.* IONIP, a criterion of surgical outcome and patient selection for perioperative nutritional support. Br J Clin Pract 1988; **42**(suppl. 63): 8-14.

26. Rana SK, Bray J, Menzies-Gow N *et al.* Short term benefits of post-operative oral dietary supplements in surgical patients. Clin Nutr 1992; **11**: 337-344.

27. Jensen JE, Jensen TG, Smith TK *et al.* Nutrition in orthopaedic surgery. J Bone Joint Surg 1982; **11**: 337-344.

28. Sullivan DH, Patch GA, Walls RC, Lipschitz DA. Impact of nutrition status on morbidity and mortality in a select population of geriatric rehabilitation patients. Am J Clin Nutr 1990; **51**: 749-758.

29. Robinson G, Goldstein M, Levine GM. Impact of nutritional status on DRG length of stay. J Parent Ent Nutr 1987; **11**: 49-51.

30. Haydock DA, Hill GL. Improved wound healing response surgical patients receiving intravenous nutrition. Br J Surg 1987; **74**: 320-323.

31. Dionigi R, Zonta A, Dominioni L *et al.* The effects of total parenteral nutrition on immunodepression due to malnutrition. Ann Surg 1988; **185**: 467-474.

32. Rana SK, Bray J, Menzies-Gow N *et al.* Short term benefits of post-operative dietary supplements in surgical patients. CLin Nutr 1992; **11**: 337-344.

33. Christie PM, Hill GL. Effect of intravenous nutrition on nutrition and function in acute attacks of inflammatory bowel disease. Gastroenterology 1990; **99**: 730-736.

34. Studley HO. Percentage of weight loss: a basic indicator of surgical risk in patients with chronic peptic ulcer.

35. The Veterans Affairs Total Parenteral Nutrition Co-operative Study Group. Perioperative total parenteral nutrition in surgical patients. N Eng J Med 1991; **35**: 525-532.

36. Compos ACL, Geguid MM. A critical appraisal of the usefulness of perioperative nutritional support. Am J Clin Nutr 1992; **55**: 117-130.

37. Delmi M, Rapin C-H, Bengoa J-M *et al.* Dietary supplementation in elderly patients with fractured neck of the femur. Lancet 1990; **335**: 1013-1016.

38. Larsson J, Unosson M, Ek A-C *et al.* Effect of dietary supplement on nutritional status and clinical outcome in 501 geriatric patients - a randomised study.

39. Cabré E, Gassull MA. Nutritional aspects of chronic liver disease. Clin Nutr 1993; **12**(suppl 1): 552-563.

40. Bowling TE, Jameson JJ, Grimble GK, Silk DBA. Enteral nutrition as a primary therapy in active Crohn's disease. Eur J Gastrol Hepatol 1993; **5**: 1-7.

41. Kudsk KA. Gut mucosal nutritional support - enteral nutrition as primary therapy after multiple system trauma. GUT 1994; **Suppl. 1**: S52-S54.

42. ASPEN Board of Directors. Guidelines for the use of parenteral nutrition in the hospitalised adult patient. JPEN 1986; **10**: 441-445.

43. Twomey PL, Patchings SC. Cost-effectiveness of nutritional support. J Parent Ent Nutr 1985; **9**: 3-10.

44. Jendteg S, Larsson J, Lindgren B. Clinical and economic aspects on nutritional supply. Clin Nutr 1987; **6**: 185-190.

45. Lennard-Jones JE (ed.). A positive approach to nutrition as treatment. Kings Fund Centre, 126 Albert St, London NW1 7NP 1992.

46. Silk DBA. Choice of enteral diets and their formulation in artificial nutrition support in clinical practice. In: Grimble GK, Payne-James JJ, Silk DBA (eds) ??? Edward Arnold, Sevenoaks, Kent, 1994: (in press).

47. Whitehouse JMA. Best documented practice. Time to set down a few benchmarks. Br Med J 1989; **289**: 1536-1537.

48. Payne-James JJ, de Gara CJ, Grimble GK *et al.* Nutritional support in hospitals in the United Kingdom: National Survey 1988. Health Trends 1990; **22.1**: 9-13.

49. Payne-James JJ, de Gara CJ, Grimble GK *et al.* Artificial nutritional support in hospital in the United Kingdom - 1991: Second National Survey. Clin Nutr 1992; **11**: 187-192.

50. Bernard RW, Stahl WM. Subclavian vein catheterisations; a prospective study. I: Non-infectious complications. Ann Surg 1971; **173**: 184-190.

51. Bernard RW, Stahl WM, Chase RM. Subclavian vein catheterisations; a prospective study. II: Infectious complications. Ann Surg 1971; **173**: 191-200.

52. Curry CR, Quie PG. Fungal septicaemia in patients receiving parenteral hyperalimentation. New Engl J Med 1971; **285**: 1221-1224.

53. Ausman RK, Hardy G. Metabolic complications of parenteral nutrition. In: Johnston, IDA (ed.) Advances in parenteral nutrition. MTP Press, Lancaster, 1978: 403-310.

54. Ellis BW, Stanbridge RdeL, Fielding LP, Dudley HAF. A rational approach to parenteral nutrition. Brit Med J 1976; **1**: 1388-1391.

55. Fleming CR, McGill DB, Hoffman HN, Nelson RA. Total parenteral nutrition. Mayo Clinic Proc 1976; **51**: 197-199.

56. Goldmann DA, Maki DG. Infection control in total parenteral nutrition. JAMA 1973; **223**: 1360-1364.

57. Ryan JA, Abel RM, Abbott WM *et al.* Catheter complication in total parenteral nutrition: a prospective study of 200 consecutive patients. Ne Engl J Med 1974; **290**: 757-761.

58. Maki DG. Sepsis arising from extrinsic contamination of the infusion and measures for control. In: Phillips I, Meers PD, D'Arcy PF (eds) Microbiological hazards of infusion therapy. MTP Press, Lancaster, 1976: 99-140.

59. Allen JR. The incidences of nosocomial infection in patients receiving total parenteral nutrition. In: Johnston IDA (ed.) Advances in parenteral nutrition. MTP Press, Lancaster, 1978: 339-377.

60. Powell-Tuck J, Neilsen T, Farwell JA, Lennard-Jones JE. Team approach to long term intravenous feeding in patients with gastrointestinal disorders. Lancet 1978; **2**: 825.

61. Sanders RA, Sheldon GF. Septic complications of total parenteral nutrition. Am J Surg 1976; **132**: 214-220.

62. Faubion WC, Wesley JR, Khalidi N, Silva J. Total parenteral nutrition catheter sepsis: impact of the team approach. JPEN 1986; **10**: 642-645.

63. Ryan Ja, Abel RM, Abbott WM *et al.* Catheter complications of total parenteral nutrition. N Engl J Med 1980; **390**: 757-760.

64. Allan A, Sellers W, Mortensen N, Leaper D. Total parenteral nutrition a team for central venous line insertion at the Bristol Royal Infirmary: results of a pilot scheme. Bristol Med Chir J 1984; **99**: 11-13.

65. Keohane PP, Jones BJ, Attrill H *et al.* Effect of catheter tunnelling and a nutrition nurse on catheter sepsis during parenteral nutrition. A controlled trial. Lancet 1983; **ii**: 1388-1390.

66. Jacobs DO, Melnik G, Forlaw L *et al.* Impact of a nutritional support service on VA surgical patients. J Am Coll Nutr 1984; **243**: 1906-1908.

67. Nehme AE. Nutritional support of the hospitalised Patient: the team concept. JAMA 1980; **243**: 1906-1908.

68. Dalton MJ, Schepers G, Gee JP *et al.* Consultative total parenteral nutrition teams: the effect on the incidence of total parenteral nutrition related complications. JPEN 1984; **8**: 146-152.

69. Shanbhogue LHR, Chwals WJ, Weintraub M *et al.* Parenteral nutrition in the surgical patient. Br J Surg 1987; **74**: 172-180.

70. Brown RO, Carlson SD, Cowan GSM *et al.* Enteral nutritional support management in a university teaching hospital, JPEN 1987; **11**: 52-56.

71. Jacobs S, Change RWS, Lee B, Bartlett FW. Continuous enteral feeding: a major cause of pneumonia among ventilated intensive care unit patients. JPEN 1990; **14**: 353-356.

72. Payne-James JJ. Infection and bacterial contamination in enteral nutrition. Riv Ital Nutr Parent Enterale 1991; **9.2**: 79-87.

73. Payne-James JJ. Are nutritional support teams justified? Current Medical Literature, Gastroenterology 1991; **10.2**: 40-43.

74. Shildt RA, Rose M. Organisation of the nutritional support service at a medical centre: one year's experience. Milit Med 1982; **147**: 55-58.

75. O'Brien DD, Hodges RE, Day AT *et al*. Recommendations of nutrition support team promotes cost containment. JPEN 1986; **10**: 300-302.

76. Friedman MH, Higa AM, Davis AJ. A unique team approach to optimal nutritional support with minimal cost. Nutr Supp Serv 1983; **3**: 27-28.

77. Puntis JWL, Holden CE, Smallman S *et al*. Staff training: a key factor in reducing intravascular catheter sepsis. Arch Dis Child 1991; **66**: 335-337.

78. Weinsier RL, Heimburger DC, Samples CM *et al*. Cost containment: a contribution of aggressive nutritional support in burn patients. J Burn Care Rehabil 1985; **11**: 436-441.

79. Traeger SM, Williams GB, Milliren G *et al*. Total parenteral nutrition by a nutrition support team: improved quality of care. JPEN 1986; **10**: 408-412.

80. Burnham WR. The role of a nutrition support team in artificial nutritional support in clinical practice. In: Artificial Nutrition Support in Clinical Practice. Editors Grimble GK, Payne-James JJ, Silk DBA. Edward Arnold, London 1994.

81. Horsphen R, Plusa SM, Kendall-Smith S *et al*. The impact of the introduction of a clinical nutrition team in the safety and efficacy of intravenous nutrition, the pivotal role of the nutrition nurse. Proc 2nd Annual Meeting BAPEN 1993.

82. Holdoway A, Simpson R, Fielden J *et al*. Nutritional needs in a District General Hospital. The Kings Fund Report in Practice. Proc 2nd Annual Meeting BAPEN 1993.

83. Askanazi J, Hensle TW, Starker PM, Lockhart SH, Lasala PA, Olssson C, Kinney JM. Effect of immediate, postoperative nutritional support on length of hospitalization. Ann Surg 1986:**203**:236-239.

84. Sagar S, Harland P, Shields R. Early post-operative feeding with elemental diet. Br Med J 1979;**1**:293-295.

85. Freeman JB, Lemire A, MacLean LD. Intravenous alimentation and septicaemia. Surg Gynec Obstet 1972;**135**:708 - 712.

NOTES